FRENCH'S

AMERICAN DRAMA.

The Acting Edition.

No. CXXVII.

"TO PARENTS AND GUARDIANS! AT JUBILEE HOUSE ESTABLISHMENT, CLAPHAM, YOUNG GENTLEMEN ARE, &c. &c."

AN

ORIGINAL COMIC DRAMA, IN ONE ACT

BY THE AUTHOR OF

"Diogenes," "The Philosopher's Stone," "The "Vicar of Wakefield," "Sir Roger de Coverley," "Red Riding Hood," &c.

TO WHICH ARE ADDED,

A Description of the Costume—Cast of the Characters—Entrances and Exits—Relative Positions of the Performers on the Stage, and the whole of the Stage Business.

AS PERFORMED AT THE NEW YORK THEATRES.

NEW-YORK:

SAMUEL FRENCH,

122 NASSAU-STREET.

Cast of the Characters.—To Parents and Guardians.

	Broadway, N. Y.	Wallack's.
Mr. Swish, Master of Jubilee House, Select Academy for Young Gentlemen,	Mr. France.	Mr. Stoddart.
Monsieur Tourbillon, the resident 'Parisian' Usher,	" Bouricault.	" H. Placide
Mas. Robt. Nettles,	Miss A. Robertson.	Mrs. Stephens
" *Wm. Waddilove*, (Pupils at the same Academy)	Mr. W. Davidge.	Mr G. Holland.
" *Skutler*,	Miss Richardson.	" Jeffries.
" *Skraggs*	" M. Osborne.	Miss Bowden.
" *Brown*,	" E. Osborne.	Mas. G. Holland.
" *Thornton*,	" Roberts.	" Holland.
" *Thompson*,	" Herbert.	" George.
" *Neville*,	Mas. Wallis.	Miss Pyne.
" *Hargrave*,	" Smith.	Mas. Charles.
" *Spencer*,	" Thomas.	Mr. Thompson.
" *Howell*,	" Davis.	" Burke.
" *Norton*,	" Hart.	" Flanry.
" *Sinclair*,	" Camp.	" Benschotten.
Doggett,	Mr. McDoual	
Nubbles, a Farmer,	" Cutter.	
Lady Nettles,	Mrs. Henry.	Mrs. Sylvester.
Mary Swish,	" J. [illegible]ugenheim.	Miss Melville.
Virginie,	" Nagle	Mrs. Conover.

STAGE DIRECTIONS.

EXITS AND ENTRANCES.

L. means *First Entrance, Left.* R. *First Entrance, Right.* S. E. L. *Second Entrance, Left.* S. E. R. *Second Entrance, Right.* U. E. L. *Upper Entrance, Left.* U. E. R. *Upper Entrance, Right* C. *Centre.* L. C. *Left of Centre.* R. C. *Right of Centre.* T. E. L *Third Entrance, Left.* T. E. R. *Third Entrance, Right.* C. D. *Centre Door.* D. R. *Door Right.* D. L. *Door Left.* U. D. L. *Upper Door, Left.* U. D. R. *Upper Door, Right.*

*** *The Reader is supposed to be on the Stage, facing the Audience.*

Costume.—To Parents and Guardians.

SWISH.—Black suit, iron-grey wig.

TOURBILLON.—Drab or grey long frock coat; black pantaloons; hessian boots; white hat, with mourning band; grey hair and bald crown;—the dress much worn, but scrupulously clean.

NETTLES.—Shooting jacket, waistcoat, trousers, and shoes, Kilmarnock cap.

BOYS.—Frocks, velveteen jackets, blouses, caps, wideawakes, &c.

WADDILOVE.—Light blue short jacket, waistcoat and trousers, boy's cap with glazed peak.

NUBBLES.—Dark blue body coat, striped waistcoat, drab breeches and gaiters.

DOGGETT.—Livery coat.

LADY NETTLES.—Fashionable carriage dress.

MARY SWISH.—White frock.

VIRGINIE.—Figured cotton dress; apron; handkerchief round neck, another round the head. Second dress: elegant silk dress.

TO PARENTS AND GUARDIANS.

SCENE I.—*An Apartment in Jubilee House—Table, with pens, ink, paper, &c., &c.*

MR. SWISH *discovered* R. C., *reading a double* "Times" *and Supplement.*

Swish. Dear, dear! the newspapers are getting so large, it will soon be impossible to find anything in them. [*Running his finger along the advertisements*] Ah! here's the scholastic column. [*Reads*] "Education—superior advantages." Ah! here's my advertisement! [*Reads*] "To Parents and Guardians—Jubilee House Establishment, Clapham. In this select academy for young gentlemen, all branches of human knowledge are communicated by a method peculiar to the principal, by which corporal punishment is rendered unnecessary." By the bye, I forgot to flog that Waddilove, this morning—he shall have twice his usual allowance to-morrow. [*Reads*]—"The diet is of the best quality, and unlimited in quantity." I've noticed that boy Skraggs regularly takes one helping of pudding and two of meat—I must reverse the arrangement. [*Reads*] "The system engenders the greatest purity of morals, and integrity of conduct." I wonder what boy it is, who is always robbing my orchard? It must be Waddilove—he's continually suffering from indigestion. [*Reads*] "Reference is kindly permitted, &c." Yes! I think that reads well—it ought to draw pupils.

Enter MARY, L. 1 E., *with skipping rope.*

Mary. Oh, Pa! here's Lady Nettles' carriage at the door—she wants to see you—here's her card.

Swish. [*Rising*] Show her ladyship in. Doggett, [*calling off* L.] show her in instantly! Come to see her son—the most troublesome young dog I ever birched into propriety.

Mary. Bob Nettles, Pa?—oh, he's a duck!

Swish. Mary, my child, how can a boy of fifteen be a duck? It's contrary to the classification of Cuvier.

Mary. [*Half aside*] Bother Cuvier! I say he *is* a duck, and I don't care!

Enter DOGGETT, *showing in* LADY NETTLES, L. 1 E.

Dog. Lady Nettles!

Swish. It is with proud humility my Lady, that I——

Lady N. [*To* MARY, *who is going*] Don't disturb yourself for me, my dear, I'd not derange anybody for the world. [*To* DOGGETT] Young man, let one of the people here take my spaniel from the carriage, and get him some white-wine whey, instantly. [*To* SWISH] Good morning, Doctor—he's ailing, poor fellow. [DOGGETT *is going*] And—young man—let one of the servants run to the Bookseller's at the end of the Crescent, on the other side of the Square, and say he may send the prints. [*Exit* DOGGETT, L. 1 E.

Swish. (C.) Will your Ladyship?——[*Brings forward chairs; they sit.*

Lady N. (L. C.) I was making a call in the neighborhood, and I thought I would look in to see my boy—my Robert—he's going on well, I hope, Doctor?

Swish. Going on well, Lady Nettles? he's going on wonderfully—tremenduously—alarmingly—always going on, [*aside*] the scamp!

Lady N. And his accomplishments, Doctor?—his dancing—does he polk?

Mary. [*Jumps up* R.] Like an angel!

Lady N. [*Eyeing her through her glass*] Eh?

Swish. [*Confused*] Oh! polks divinely—he has created quite an enthusiasm in the establishment. Mary, my child, retire, and order refreshments. [*Exit* MARY, L. 1 E.

Lady N. Delightful! Because, as he's intended for the army, of course he must dance.

Swish. Of course!—preliminary ball practice.

Lady N. And his manners—still the same timid retiring creature?

Swish. A leetle less shy. [*Aside*] The most impudent rascal in the establishment. I've caught him making love to the cook on three separate occasions.

Lady N. Still averse to violent exercise?

Swish. On the contrary—active—decidedly active. [*Aside*] Tumbled last week, through Doctor Squill's conservatory, next door, in an attempt to steal his Jargonels.

Lady N. Beloved by his schoolfellows?

Swish. Adored! [*Aside*] Fights two battles a day on a low average.

Lady N. And esteemed by his teachers?

Swish. Held up as an example. [*Aside*] He has been twice detected sticking cobbler's wax to the writing master's pantaloons.

Lady N. Your account of him is most gratifying to my feelings as a mother. As he is intended for the army, Sir John and I both shrunk from the idea of a public school. But I'm all impatience to see the dear boy—where is he?

Swish. [*Aside*] I wish I had known she was coming. [*Aloud*] I'll let him know, my Lady. [*Offers to rise.*

Lady N No, no, Doctor, I want to surprise him—to enjoy his delight at the unexpected visit of his mamma.

Swish. [*Aside*] Hang it! [*Aloud*] Your Ladyship shall be gratified.

[*Aside*] I hope he's fit to be seen. [*Aloud*] This is one of our hours of healthful recreation.

Enter DOGGETT, L. 1 E., *with wine, &c., which he places on table.*

—Doggett, present my respects to Master Robert Nettles, and beg him to walk into this apartment, if he is disengaged.

Dog [*Aside—crossing behind to* R.] How uncommon civil the governor is. It used to be "Fetch Nettles!" [*Exit,* R. 1 E.

Swish. Yes, your Ladyship will find no vicious, low, brutal dispositions are encouraged in this establishment—no fighting—no violence——

[*Noise outside,* R.

Net. [*Outside*] Shan't, I tell you!

Dog. [*Without*] You must! Here's young Nettles!

Enter DOGGETT R. 1 E., *dragging in* ROBERT NETTLES, *his nose bleeding, his collar torn, his jacket half off, and his whole dress in disorder.*

Lady N. My boy! Oh, heavens!

Net. [*Aside*] Oh my!—if it ain't ma!

Swish. [*Aside*] Confound the young rascal, he's been fighting again.

Lady N. I shall faint!

Net. Ah, ma!—take a refresher! [*Goes to table and pours out wine*] something strong and short. [*Offers glass*

Lady N. Away, bold, bad boy!

[NETTLES *drinks the wine him*

Swish. Master Robert, my dear boy, speak to your excellent mother. [*Aside*] Put down that glass, you young rascal, or I will flay you alive!

Net. (R) I say, ma, don't be frightened, I'm not hurt, it was all Skutler—he would stick pins into Waddilove—and as Waddilove's my fag, of course I wasn't going to let anybody bully him but myself; and so I and Skutler had a regular set-to. I wish you could see the black eye he's got.

Lady N (L.) Fighting with a low boy called Skutler! Oh, Doctor Swish, you have deceived me! I had intended to have taken our unhappy child home with me, but the spectacle I have seen has given me such a shock, I can't bear the sight of him. Good morning, Doctor Swish, I shall consult Sir John on the propriety of removing our lost child from your charge. [NETTLES *advances towards her*] Don't come near me, dirty, dreadful boy—quarrelling and fighting—you'll be a disgrace to the army. [*Exit* LADY NETTLES, L.

Swish. But, your Ladyship—[*to* NETTLES] I'll come back and flog you, you rascal! [*Exit* SWISH, L.

Net. Well, I don't care—women don't understand lark, except Mary Swish. I believe I'm in love with Mary. I am almost sure I am. [*Sits* R. *of table*] I couldn't eat more than one helping of pudding yesterday, because I saw her wink at Clump as we came from church. Mary gives me potatoes, browned in the dripping-pan, and she lets me see the newspaper before old Swish gets it. I wish the old chap would take in *Bell's Life*, the *Times* is so precious slow. By the bye, I saw something about old Tourbillon, in the *Times*, this morning. Ah, here it is!—[*Reading*] "If any person can give any information respecting Count

Victor Amédée de Rocheguyon de Tourbullion, who is supposed to have come to England some years back, it will be thankfully received by Messrs. Mortmain and Twigg, 14, Chancery Lane; or, if this meets the eye of the said Count V. A. de R. de T., he will, on applying at the above address, hear of something very greatly to his advantage." Well, I'm glad of it! I've written to uncle George, in the Temple, to make enquiries for me. I hope it's all spelt right, or I shan't get the squibs I want. [*Reads*] "My dear uncle George"——Ah, there's a mistake at starting! I've spelt uncle with a C, instead of a K. "My dear uncle George—I am very well, and I hope you are well. I am getting on very well with my French, but I do not like Latin. We have a half-holiday to-morrow. If you please to read the fourth advertisement from the top of the second column of the *Times* to-day, and go and enquire, and say that I know the party, and he is a French usher here, and very much bullied by Doctor Swish and the fellows; but *we* do it only in fun, and I wish to surprise him with the news. He will be so much surprised to hear anything pleasant from me. So, my dear uncle, I remain, your affectionate nephew, Robert Nettles. P.S. Do you know when I am to leave school? I don't think I have much to learn, and I should like very much to be in the army. P.S. As we are forbidden to buy squibs, I wish you'd send me down a pound of gunpowder to make some. P.S. We are all obliged to eat fat." Nasty beasts!—large lumps of fat, enough to make one shiver in one's shoes. There, that will do. One of the day boys will post it, and I'll have an answer to-day. [*Looking off*, L. 1 E.] Hallo! There's old Swish laying all the blame of our fight upon old Tourbillon. The old boy's a great deal more of a gentleman than Swish. I wonder what he's been! I often catch him looking as if he was fit to cry, with a picture in his hand. I'm sorry for the poor fellow, but one can't help bullying the French master. Hallo! here's Mary!

Enter MARY, L. 1 E.

Mary. Oh! Bob, your ma's talking to my pa. She's in a terrible way about you, Bob!

During BOB *and* MARY'S *dialogue, they eat between them a large pear which* BOB *takes from the pocket of his jacket.*

Net. I'm in a terrible way about you, Mary. Why did you wink at Clump, yesterday?

Mary. Clump? I wink at Clump? Such a child. I didn't, Bob.

Net. (C.) Then, who did you wink at?

Mary. Well, Bob, if I *did* wink, it was at you.

Net. At me, Mary? Oh, how jolly! Do you know, Mary, I think I'm in love with you.

Mary. (R. C.) Oh, Bob, don't!

Net. It's no use saying don't. I can't help it. I'll go upon my knees. [*Kneels.*

Mary. Oh, how nice! But you'd better get up, Bob: pa will catch you.

Net. I say, you're in love, too, Mary; ain't you? Just say.

Mary. Well, I don't know, Bob; but now you put it into my head, I think I am, rather. Oh, Bob! isn't it dreadful?

Net. Horrid! I say, Mary, wouldn't it be good fun to go straight off, and get married?

Mary. Delightful! But the clergyman wouldn't marry us: we're not of age.

Net. I've a sovereign left of ma's last tip. We'll run away to Gretna Green: they'll marry anybody there.

Swish. [*Without*.] But I say it is your fault, sir!

Mary. Oh, here's pa!

Net. Remember, Mary, you've promised me your hand.

Mary. Yes; but pa will catch us.

Net. Very true. It wouldn't be the thing to be birched by one's father-in-law! Come along. [*They run off*, R. 1 E.

Enter SWISH *and* TOURBILLON, L. 1 E.

Swish. Nonsense! You had no business to let the boys fight.

Tour. I did not let dem; dey fight demselves.

Swish. You should inspire them with respect.

[*Takes snuff*. TOURBILLON *is about to take a pinch*; SWISH *closes the box*.

Tour. I try very hard.

Swish. It was your duty to keep order, sir.

Tour. Dis donc how I shall keep him, sir? All is tranquil; I walk myself in reading my Virgile, pouf!—sudden, I recognize a noise. I run up, and I see dat enragé of a Nettles, and dat diable de Skutler, who bleed to demselves de nose! knock to demselves de eye! I cry in vain. I put myself in ze middle. Vlin!—I obtain a stroke in de estomac from de one; vlan!—I catch a blow of my nose from ze oder! And, den, you say to me: "Que diable! you not keep order!" Ah, bah!

Swish. Let me tell you, sir! this tone ain't the thing! People shouldn't forget whom they are speaking to!

Tour. C'est ça! dey should not! Ainsi, do you, Monsieur, remember it?

Swish. Hallo! here's pretty behavior in a fellow I pay twenty pounds a year to, and washing extra. Remember your position, or—

Tour. [*Bitterly*.] Pardon, Monsieur, I do remember him. Je suis, usher—ze poor devil, who teach little boys to be gentlemen; but must not nevair imagine him gentleman himself. No, Monsieur Swish, you take care I nevair can forget my position!

Swish. Ah, you think that's very fine, and devilish satirical, I dare say! I must consult *your* feelings, must I? Much you thought of mine, when you nearly lost me the best pupil in my establishment. It won't do, I can tell you!

Tour. [*Restraining himself with an effort*.] Après!

Swish. I'll have no cats that don't catch mice in Jubilee House, I can tell you! If you ain't fit to do my duties, you ain't fit to receive my salary. So, I give you—

Tour. [*Stopping him*.] Halte là! Monsieur Swiss. I give *you* warning! It is too long I have support the insolences of a brutal like yourself:

dey almost have break my heart; but not all, indeed, destroy my courage. I discharge you, Monsieur le Docteur Swiss. Here I shall stay no longer; pas un moment! Je pars! And, zo I should want a morsel of bread to feed my mouse, or a clothes to put to me upon ze back, I shall, at least, presevere to me ze honor, widout a spot, of ze Rocheguyon!

[*Exit*, L. 1 E.

Swish. An impertinent, beggarly foreigner! to insult me in my own establishment! What things will come to, in these levelling times, I cannot form the remotest anticipation.

DOGGETT *enters*, L. 1 E., *and gives him a letter.*

Marked "Private and immediate." It's my agent's hand. [*Opens it.*] What's he in such a hurry about? [*Reads.*] "My dear sir; I recommended to you, some eight months ago, a French Master, a Refugee, who calls himself Monsieur de Tourbillon—" Yes, and a precious conceited old fool you recommended—"If he is still in your establishment, send him up to me directly—" With the greatest pleasure; but not carriage paid. Eh? What's this?—"A nobleman, le Comte de Rocheguyon, and the owner of large estates, which were appropriated by the Convention, and have just been recovered by the representative of the family in France." A nobleman, and rich! How very sorry I am we should have had those few words together. I feel I was in the wrong. Doggett, beg Monsieur Tourbillon to walk this way. Be extremely respectful in your manner, Doggett.

[*Exit* DOGGETT, L.

How very interesting! I always thought he looked above his situation. Quite the gentleman. I'll apologize to him for my hasty expressions. I'll beg him to stay. I'll offer him a partnership in the school. What, if I could get him to marry Mary? Engraft the French fleur de lys on the British birch. Egad! I'll try it. So, for the present, not a word of this letter, and the change in his prospects!

Enter TOURBILLON, L. 1 E., *with a small bundle in a pocket-handkerchief, an umbrella under his arm.* SWISH *seizes him eagerly by the hand.*

My dear sir, allow me to apologize for my hasty and violent language. I was wrong, my dear Monsieur Tourbillon; but I was in a passion. Ira est brevis—hum!—but you'll forgive me. I know the excellence of your heart; you'll forgive me.

Tour. Assez—enough, Monsieur Swiss: I accept your reparation. [*Aside.*] He is, then, a noble heart, dis Swiss.

Swish. And all is forgotten?

Tour. Tout!

Swish. You'll continue at Jubilee House?

Tour. Mais certainement.

Swish. Allow me to put down your bundle. [*He places it on table.*] One learns the value of things in losing 'em. I've just found out how much you were worth. [*Aside.*] That's true, at all events. [*Aloud.*] Permit me to take charge of your umbrella. [*Puts it on table.*] I feel we ought to be more closely connected. Give me leave to take your hat. [*Puts it down.*] You'll dine with me, to-day, my dear Sir?

Tour. Monsieur! [*Aside.*] He is a generous!

Swish. I think you'd better not sleep any longer in the dormitory; you shall have a separate bed-room.

Tour. Monsieur! [*Aside.*] He is a noble!

Swish. You must no longer be troubled with the charge of the boys out of school.

Tour. Monsieur! [*Aside.*] He is an extravagant!

Swish. As soon as possible, I'll make arrangements for admitting you into partnership.

Tour. Monsieur! [*Aside.*] He is a dronk!

Swish. And, such is my regard for you, you shall marry my daughter.

Tour. Monsieur!!! Ah! [*Aside*] I can no more: he is a mad!

Swish. [*Offers snuff.*] Allow me to offer you a pinch. Meanwhile, I am obliged to run up to town; I leave you in full and uncontrolled authority over Jubilee House establishment.

Tour. Mais—it is a confidence!

Swish. Which you deserve. Good morning, my dear sir. [*Aside.*] Now, to tell Mary to receive Tourbillon as her intended.

Tour. Un moment, Monsieur!—Suppose, during your absence, dat dey shall box demselves?

Swish. Separate them.

Tour. But if I sall not can to separate dem?

Swish. Let them fight it out, and separate them afterwards.

Tour. But suppose dey go for swim, and drown demselves?

Swish. Don't risk your precious life by attempting to save them! [*Exit*, L.

Tour. Ah! I ask you, is it not a beautiful prospect, to control, for an only day, dese rascals of leetle boys? Que diable arrive to Swiss, dat he change of tone to me tout d'un coup? But what a proposal! It is too strong! Dine wiz you?—yes! Sleep in a room all alone to myself?—avec plaisir! Become a half of Jubilee House?—wiz all my heart! But marry your daughter?—oh, que non! [*Sits*, R. *of table.*] Marry?—me, dat am marry to de recollection of her dat I have loved and lost—to a memory of de past, dat have become my hope of de future? Mon dieu! when I think how it is now fifteen year dat we part à Paris—dat scene of blood, of horror! It must be dat she perish, ma femme! ma bien aimée! But our child, dey could not kill her! If she live, she will now be like to her mother, ma Virginie! [*Looks at portrait.*] Et toi, ma Virginie! [*Kisses it.*] What say you of it, ma bien aimée? Toujours à moi! à ton Victor! n'est-ce pas?

Enter NETTLES, *softly*, R.

Net. There he is. What has he got there? It's that portrait I've never got a good peep at it. [*Peeping.*] Oh, my!—what a pretty woman! [TOURBILLON *kisses the miniature.*] Oh, fie, old gentleman! [*Coughs.*] Doesn't hear me. I hope it's his wife. [TOURBILLON *kisses miniature again.*] Oh, he's going too far! Hem!

[*Coughs very loud.* TOURBILLON *starts from his reverie, and hastily conceals portrait.*

Net. (R. C.) Please, sir, I've come to say I'm very sorry that I pitched into Skutler, to-day, and got you into a row. Please, sir, I beg your pardon.

Tour. I do not remember noting. Adieu, mon petit ami!

[*Exit slowly*, L.

Net. More melo-dramatic than polite. Never mind, I have done the handsome thing; and, now, I'll be off, and thrash Skutler.

[*Exit*, R.

SCENE II.—*Play-Ground at Jubilee House.—A wall across at back, with iron gate*, C., *having spikes at the top.—Stone porch with door*, R. 3 E.—SKUTLER, SCRAGGS, *and* BOYS *playing at marbles and other games.*

Skra. (L.) Knuckle down.

Sku. (L. C.) Two out!

Skra. It's a take in!—play fair, can't you?

Sku. Just you call me a cheat again!

Skra. I didn't call you a cheat—I only said it was a take in.

Sku. You'd better not say it again—that's all!

Skra. Ah, you're very plucky, now Bob Nettles isn't in the play-ground.

NETTLES *enters*, R. 3 E.

Sku. Bob Nettles!—oh, I like that. We didn't fight it out this morning, or I'd have soon let him see——

Net. [C., *coming forward, turning up his sleeves.*] Eh!—let him see?

Sku. That I didn't bear any malice, and had no objection to shake hands and make it up.

Net. Well, I don't mind. You're an ass *in præsenti*, perhaps you'll be wise *in futuro*. [*Shakes hands.*] Where's Waddilove?

Skra. Oh, he hasn't come back yet, Bob.

Net. I hope he has not forgotten any of my commissions.

A DOG *is heard to bark*, R. U. E.; *they go up and open the gate;* WADDILOVE *runs on, loaded with packages, bottles, &c.*

Wad. Here, take the things; there's good fellows. I've got the eggs; but—[DOG *barks.*]—Here's old Nubbles coming after me with his bull dog.

Net. (R. C.) There!—what a short-winded old stupid it is.

Wad. (C.) Ah, I knew how it would be!—sending me after those eggs in old Nubbles' field. If you must have new-laid eggs, I wish you'd go poaching 'em yourself.

Net. Waddilove, you're ungrateful! Waddy, you're insolent! Waddy, you're rebellious! [*Doubling his fist.*] I must do it!

Wad. Well, Bob, half a mile run's no joke, with a ferocious dog nibbling about the skirts of one's jacket! I felt his teeth in me! I shouldn't wonder if I take the hydrophobia—if I do, won't I bite! that's all!

Net. Yes; and won't we smother you between two feather beds! Did you get the pale ale?

Wad. Here it is; but the man says he won't give any more trust to the Jubilee House boys in general, and Master Robert Nettles in parti cular; so, I was forced to pay for it; I couldn't help it. I wouldn't have paid, Bob, but I couldn't get it without.

Net. I'm not angry, Waddy; quite the reverse: I'm delighted to see you go on the ready money principle.

Wad. Yes! but as it is for *your* drinking, you know——

Net. Yes; for our drinking. [*They put the bottles down,* R.

Wad. And I've paid for it.

Net. You're too kind! You've paid for it, as it was for our drinking? There's generosity! Waddy makes us a present of the pale ale.

Omnes. Thank you, Waddy! [*They all shake hands with him.*

Wad. But I didn't mean——

Net. To drink any of it yourself?—of course not. Waddy, you're an ornament to your sex. Got the cigars for me?

Wad. They were out of penny Pickwicks; so, I've brought half-penny Bengals. [*Aside.*] I wish Nettles would give me some money when he sends me out to buy things.

Net. Hum—ha—yes! I think they'll do.

Wad. But hadn't I better get the eggs out of my pocket?

Net. Why, yes! In case I should have to pitch into you, I might hurt the eggs.

Wad. I've been so nervous about these eggs, you can't think; the old hen herself couldn't have been more excited on the subject. [*Taking out the eggs, and handing them to the boys, who put them into* WADDY'S *hat; he dives to the bottom of his trowsers pocket, and is horrified at feeling the eggs cracked.*] There, I knew how it would be!—here are two of them smashed, all among the toffy.

Net. You may eat those yourself: they're good for the wind, and I like to reward industry. [*Looking over parcels.*] Ah! here are all the squibs, I see, and the novels from the circulating library—all about love and murder.

Wad. [*Aside.*] Now, I'll go and stow away in my box the jolly big cake I bought for myself. [*Exit,* R. 3 E.

Sku. Oh! shan't we have a tuck-in, to-night, in the bed-room?

Net. (C.) Skutler, you're a horribly greedy fellow!—Isn't he?

Omnes. Horrid!

Net. I vote Skutler shan't be allowed to sup with us, to-night.

Sku. Then, I'll tell old Swish.

Net. You'd better, you mean little rascal I vote that we cob Skutler for threatening to peach!

Omnes. Hurrah! [*They seize* SKUTLER.

Enter WADDILOVE, R. 3 E.

Wad. I've stowed away the cake in my box all safe!—won't I walk into it after dark!

Net. Stop! release the culprit: we must get these things put away, or old Snuffy will be finding us out. Let's see. Ah! I have it!—wait a moment; and mind, don't you let Waddilove get at the eggs. [*Exit,* R. 3 E.

Wad. What a lively boy Nettles is, and so fond of me. He can't bear to let anybody else go his errands, or black his boots. The orchards we've robbed together, to be sure! He always makes me climb over for the apples, while he waits outside. He says he can't be comfortable unless he's watching over me. I know that apple stealing is sinful. and I believe I should be transported if I was caught; but I havn't the heart to say no to him; coz, when I do, he wops me. But, then, he doesn't let anybody else wop me, and I am of a grateful turn of mind. There's one habit of his I do not like: using me as a warming-pan in the cold nights, to take the chill off his bed, before he turns into it.

Enter NETTLES, *dragging a box; he puts it down,* C.

Net. Now, then, Waddy, look sharp, and lend us your key.

Wad Why, that's my box!

Net. Of course, it is, or I shouldn't want your key! Now, then.

Wad. [*Aside.*] They'll find the cake. [*Aloud.*] I shan't.

Net. Waddilove, my dear boy —

W[illegible] [illegible].) I shan't!

Net. Oh, Waddy! [*Turning up his cuffs.*] I think you said you wouldn't?

Wad. Well, Bob! I did say I wouldn't; but I didn't mean anything.

Net. I know you didn't; you never do. [WADDILOVE *gives key;* NETTLES *opens box.*] Hallo!—what's this? [*Brings out cake.*] A most tremendous and indigestible plum-cake! My dear Waddy, what a delicate way of giving us an agreeable surprise! Three cheers for the generous Waddilove, and one cheer more for plummy!

Omnes. Hurrah!

[NETTLES *cuts up and distributes the cake, passing* WADDILOVE; *when all are supplied, one piece remains.*

Net. Once round, and a distance. [*Takes second piece himself.*] Delicious!

Wad. I say, give us the odd piece! do, Bob!

Net. Don't be indelicate, Waddy.

Wad. Hallo!—what's that in the cake?

Net. Where?

Wad. There!

[*Pretending to point it out, he snatches a piece, and bolts up the stage, eating it.*

Net. Now, let's stow all these things away in this box.

Wad. But they're all forbidden in the school, and if they're found in my box——Suppose you put them into somebody else's box for once?—your own? now.

Net. [*Puts all the things into box.*] Now, then, be off with your box.

Wad. I can't lift it. Not content with ruining my character, you want to break my back.

Net. I'll help you, Waddy. [*They take up the box.*] At least, a hundred weight of contraband.

Wad. I believe I'm what the "History of England" calls a martyr.

[*Exeunt with the box,* R. 3. E.

Sku. I say, as Swish is gone out, I vote we aggravate old Tourbillon

Skra. Hallo! here he comes. Who's he got with him?

Sku. By Jove!—it's Nubbles the farmer, after his eggs.

Enter TOURBILLON *and* NUBBLES, C., *from* R.

Tour. (L.) C'est impossible! mon cher Monsieur Nobiles.

Nub. (C.) Nubbles! I tell you.

Tour. C'est çà! Nobiles. Ah çà, coquins! which is it of ... who rob his eggs, to ce pauvre Nobiles? Voyons! [BOYS *advance*, R., *in a line*.] You see him, Nobiles?

Nub. I seed 'un sharp enough. A fat young chap, in a wery short jacket; and there ought to be some holes somewhere, for Crib had hold of 'un.

Tour. [*Crosses to* R. C.] Range yourselves, coquins! Ah, c'est lui! dis spoiled child of a Skutler! Ah, you suck eggs! Ah!——

Nub. No!—t'other was fatter than this chap. I know it was one of your chaps as took 'em—sixteen beauties—a chicken in every one—half hatched, some of 'em.

Sku. (R. C.) [*Aside.*] I'm glad I didn't try one.

Tour. Mais. mon dieu! Nobiles—when a man lay his eggs in de open field, dey sall perhaps be stolen—c'est naturel! He is not here, eh? [*Leading him up*, C.

Nub. (C.) No!—he ain't. I daresay you're a-hiding of the young rascal. I'll fetch a police. You're all of you in it—one as bad as another.

Tour. (L.) Hold!—listen to me, Monsieur Nobiles. You come here to find your eggs!—your eggs is not here. You come here to find de tief!—de tief is not here. I commence to tink dere is no tief at all! dat you lay no eggs at all, Nobiles!

Nub. But I tell you I have, Mr. Parleyvoo!

Tour. Comment! "Parlez-vous?" Ah, you insult me! grande goddam!

Nub. Who are you a-swearing at, you hignorant foreigner?

Tour. Ignorant? Ah, retire yourself! if you would not that I should conduct you by ze nose.

Nub. You'd better!

Boys. Hurrah! [*Hustling* NUBBLES *off at gate.*

Tour. Ah, c'est bien! I respire once more. But suppose he have lost his eggs; it is one of dese coquins take dem. Voyons donc. Ici, marauds! [*Counts.*] Un—deux—trois—

As he counts, NETTLES *enters, and gets to the top of the line*, R.

Skutler—Nettles.—Oui, there wants one. Ah, mon Dieu! Mais c'est une inspiration! C'est lui!—c'est ce rascal of a Waddilove, who have sucked de eggs to Nobiles.

Enter WADDILOVE; *he skulks up to top of line*, R.; *he is seized by* TOURBILLON.

Ah, voyons!—what is behind you in your pantalon?

Wad. Eh?—what? Nothing!

Tour. [*Turning him round.*] Ah, you call dat noting?—mais moi, I call him someting! I call him a great deal too moche: de bites of a dog! Ah, you steal de eggs!—eh!

Wad. Please, sir, what is an egg?

Tour. Maraud! turn out to me your pockets!

[WADDILOVE *turns out his pockets one by one; at last, he reluctantly turns out pocket of his trousers. Some pieces of egg-shell fall out.*

Wad. Hallo!—who's been putting eggs into my pockets?

Tour. Ah, voleur! you sall to the Lord Mayor for dis.

Wad. Oh, lord, sir! don't talk so! I couldn't help it!—I was made to——

Tour. Par exemple! But when I sall soon after tell Monsieur Swiss——

Wad. Oh, Bob!

Tour. Soyez tranquil! When Docteur Swiss shall know all, I sall not choose to be in your pantalon. [*Going.*

Wad. [*Looks imploringly at* NETTLES.] Oh, Bob!

Net. [illegible] c.] Please, sir, it wasn't Waddy stole the eggs—that is, it was Waddy stole 'em; but he'd much rather not, if I hadn't made him do it.

Tour. Ah!

Net. So, if you please, sir, if you'd report me to the Doctor, I'm the boy that ought to be flogged or expelled, sir. I am, indeed, I'm the wicked boy.

Tour. [*Aside.*] It makes me joy at de heart! [*Aloud.*] Ah, you are de wicked boy!—eh? Bien, my leetle friend, you have act like a— [*Kindly, but checking himself, and aside.*] Non! de la rigueur [*Aloud.*] Like a rascal! and I sall have great plaisir of seeing you both together on the flog-horse.

Net. Please, Monsieur, don't tell.

Tour. Arriere, coquin! [*Aside*] Noble little heart! I was like dat at his age. [*Exit* L.

Sku. Shabby old wretch!

Net. Well, that's too bad!—I've gone and got myself into the scrape without getting Waddy out of it. I did think old snuffy was more of a gentleman.

Enter MARY, R. 3 E.

Boys. Oh, here's Mary!

All crowd round her—SKUTLER *comes very near and intrudes his attentions.*

Mary. (R. C.) Get away, Skutler, do. [NETTLES *boxes his ears*] Thank you, Bob—dear, dear Bob—oh, I'm in such a way!

Net. (C.) What's the matter? [*To* BOYS] Stand back!

Mary. Pa sent for me before he went to town, to tell me he wants me to marry——

Net. Who—me?

Mary. No!—Monsieur Tourbillon!

Net. Oh, by Jove!—oh, by jingo! Marry you to an old chap whose English is as broken as his teeth—marry you!—I've no doubt he's married already, and now I recollect—that portrait I caught him kissing this morning—I'll be bound it's a wife he's left behind him in France.

Mary. Oh, but these Frenchmen don't care how many wives they have—Bluebeard was a Frenchman—it says so in Guy's questions.

Net. Never mind, I'll make the school too hot to hold him. Here, you fellows, I want to make Tourbillon's life a burden to him—will you help me?

Omnes. Yes, Bob!

Net. Then from this day forth he mustn't have a moment's peace. Sew up the sleeves of his dressing gown——

Skra. Stick pins in his chair——

Sku. And devils in his snuff-box.

Net. That's right!—and if all this isn't enough, I'll bring his wife over from France, by way of a settler. [*Exit with* MARY, R. 3 E.

VIRGINIE *appears at the gate* C. *from* R., *she is dressed as a vagrant, and carries a tambourine: she sings a bar of a French song as she advances through the gate.*

Sku. Oh, here's a French girl—what a lark!

Skra. Oh, my—what a guy!

Vir. (*Up* C.) Charité, my good leetle gentlemans, for a poor leetle orphiline, widout fader or moder. I sing you pretty song. [*Sings.*

SKUTLER *imitates her—all burst out laughing but* WADDILOVE, *who gazes earnestly upon her.*

—Oh, do not mock yourselves at me, I am very tired and very sad—I sall go.

Sku. [*Getting between her and the gate*] Oh no, you don't, till you give us a caper and a tune on your thingumbob. [*All get around her.*

Wad. The low, unfeeling brutes! I say, you'd better not aggravate the girl, or——

Sku What'll you do?

Skra. Hadn't you better set up a tambourine of your own?

Omnes. Ha, ha, ha!

Vir. Oh, mon dieu!—mon dieu!

Wad. Oh, I wish I could fight!—but I'm so short of breath. I'll fetch Bob Nettles—he'll astonish you—you low, vulgar boys, he will. [*Exit,* R. 3 E.

Sku. You must dance, I tell you.

Vir. Oh, I'm too fatiguée, and too frightful—indeed—indeed!

Sku. Well, if you won't dance without a partner—here goes for a pas de deux. [*Seizes her by the hands, the rest form a ring round them.*

Enter WADDILOVE, NETTLES, *and* MARY—*as* SKUTLER *pulls* VIRGINIE *round,* NETTLES *seizes him and whirls him across stage.*

Net. Don't be afraid, little girl.

Vir. Oh, tank you—tank you!

Net. And as for you, Skutler, if I don't give you the soundest thrashing you ever had in your life, it's because it's not the thing to fight before ladies.

Sku. Well, we wern't going to hurt the girl, were we?

Omnes. No!

Sku. (L. C.) And I tell you what it is—we won't stand being bullied by you.

Omnes. No.

Sku. (C.) So you just stand out of the way, will you, and let us have our dance. [*All advance towards* BOB.

Vir. (R C.) [*Clinging to* MARY.] Oh! Mademoiselle, you will protect me—will you not?

Net. [*To* VIRGINIE] Don't be afraid. [*To* BOYS] I won't ask for fair play—fellows that would teaze and frighten a poor little girl, don't know what fair play is. Come on half-a-dozen of you to me and Mary—Waddy doesn't count.

Wad. (R.) Don't I though. [*Puts himself in attitude.*

Skra. [*To* SKUTLER] Well—why don't you go in?

Sku. Why don't *you.*

Net. Come on—I'm waiting for you.

Wad. Yes—we're waiting for you.

Vir. Oh! dey will fight—you will be hurt for me—I will dance—I will sing—but do not fight.

Mary. Oh! pray, Bob, don't go and get a black eye.

Sku. Hang it, Nettles! you are right, and we're all of us wrong. Shake hands.

Net. There! [*They shake hands.*

Wad. Yes—there—we don't bear malice—we forgive you.

[*Thrusting his hand into* SKUTLER'S

Net. Mind, the next time you bully any one, let it be a man, instead of a woman, and remember, in the words of Dr. Watts :—

Tom Skutler, you should never let
  Your angry passions rise;
Your little hands were never made
  To black Bob Nettles' eyes.

—Now, be off with you. [*All the* BOYS *exeunt,* U. E. L.

Vir. (R. C.) Ah! how he is noble—how he is courageux! How sall I tank you?—I will sing you a song, it is all I can—for I am so poor—so poor.

Wad. (R.) What an interesting creature! [*Gives money*] Here my poor, pretty French girl—it is all I've got; I wish I'd seen you before I bought that cake.

Vir. Tank you, my kind gentleman. [*They go up.*

Net. (L.) Mary, I'm nearly certain old Tourbillon's left a wife behind him—now as we can't go to France for the genuine article, here's this little French girl—suppose we dress her up, and set her on the old fellow as Mrs. Tourbillon.

Mary. (L. C.) Oh! let's try it—I've the French bonnet and pelisse papa bought me, when we were at Boulogne. But will *she* consent to the trick?

Net. She looks too tired and hungry to be very particular. I say—do you speak English?

Vir. [*Comes* C.] Oh! yes—it is so long dat I wander in England, I speak nothing but English. I speak him so 'andsome, all de world tink me English girl.

Net. (R. C.) No doubt of it. Would you like to earn five shillings?

Vir. Oh! it is so moche money, I will sing you ever so many of chansons for dat. [*Sings*—NETTLES *stops her.*

Wad. (R.) Oh! don't stop her—it's beautiful—it does me good—its a petit chanson d'amore.

Net. [*To* VIRGINIE] What's your name?

Vir. Dey call me Virginia—noting more, Virginie.

Wad. It's a sweet name—so musical—Virginie!

Net. Then look here, Virginie—we've a lark going on here—a lark—you understand?

Vir. Lark? Lark? what is he, Lark? Ah! oui, I understand—de leetle bird dat sing—so high—so high—I not see him, no more—but I hear his sweet voice, and den I forget dat I am fatiguée, and dance along as merry as his music.

Wad. It's the skylark she means, Bob.

Net. [*Giving him a dig with his elbow*] Just hold your tongue, Waddy—you're a nuisance.

Wad. It's most affecting to hear her—I'll go and have a good cry where my feelings won't be insulted. [*Exit* R. 3 E.

Net. We're playing at a game. What's the French for game? Oh, I know. C'est un gibier!

Vir. Not de lark—he is not "gibier"

Net. Dear, dear! how stupid these foreigners are. We want you to dress yourself up—and pretend to be a gentleman's wife.

Vir. [*Alarmed*] Mais—comment—oh!

Net. Oh! he's an old gentleman—you'll only have to rush into his arms, you know, and——

Vir. Par exemple! Oh! I cannot! [*goes* L.

Net. [*Crosses to* C.] You needn't mind—he's dreadfully ugly—and I dare say he'll fight remarkably shy of you. So be off, Mary, and dress up Virginie. I'll tip Doggett to bring her in at the proper time, and just humbug cook to give her something to eat—will you?

Vir. Oh! you are full of goods for me, mon bon Monsieur. Oh! how much I tank you. [*Exit with* MARY, R. 3 E.

A bell rings—BOYS *all re-enter*, U. E. L.

Net. There's the two o'clock bell—off into school with you all—we'll soon teach the Frenchman what it is to rouse the British Lion. [*Exeunt* R. 3 E.

SCENE III.—*Room in Jubilee House.*

Enter WADDILOVE, *with a Book in his hand, eating toffy*, R. 1 E.

Wad. I can't do any good in school; so I managed to slip out, when old Tourbillon wasn't looking, to have a little solitary reflection, and a tuck-in at toffy. That poor little French girl—I've not been easy in my mind, since I saw her—I can't learn any lessons—the only thing I *can* do, is to conjugate the verb "aimer"—to love, with the advantage of all the auxiliaries. [*Conjugating*] "J'aimé," I love!—"J'auris aimé," I should have loved—if I hadn't been afraid of Nettles—"Tu aurais aimé," thou—that's you, Virginie—mightst, couldst, wouldst, or shouldst have loved—if you'd known the turn you gave me—"Ils auraient aimé," they might, could, would, or should have loved—if they hadn't been low boys, without the least sentiment. I only wish my coat was come home—I think I should feel more confidence, out of my short jacket. Here comes the interesting orphan.

Enter MARY *and* VIRGINIE, R.

Mary. (R.) And so your mother's dead?

Vir. (R. C.) Helas—oui!—dead of break de heart—my fader was Royaliste in ze Revolution—he fly to save his life, wisout to tell her his place of refuge. She seek to find and join him—Helas, in vain—she pine and pine, and die of grief, before my eye, and leave her poor Virginie alone—alone. Wid her last breath she charge me come to England, where she hope I find Papa. I try to come—but alone—wisout money—wisout friend, à Dunkirk, I fall sick into an inn—dere kind English lady give me help, and send me to dis country, where I wander now many, many year. I sing my leetle song—I always feel de hope to find Papa—but always dat hope deceive me. Mais pardon, I talk too much.

Wad. [*Who is much affected, comes forward.*] Oh, no, poor French girl, go on—pray go on—it's like a novel.

Mary. Yes, and true into the bargain. I'm almost ashamed of Bob's trick. Come along, Virginie, you'll look charming in my new dress.

Wad. I say, orphan, I can speak French—"J'aime"—I love—"Aimes tu"—dost thou love?

Vir. [*Laughing.*] Is he droll?—ze leetle fat.

[*Exit with* MARY, D. *in* F. R. C.

Wad. Fat! Oh, why haven't I what Nettles calls a prepossessing exterior? I'm sure I ain't very fond of French grammar, but I could stay conjugating the verb "Aimer"—to love, with the orphan, all day long. "J'aime"—I love—oh, don't I!

Enter NETTLES, R. 1 E.

Net. Where's Mary?

Wad. Gone to disguise the orphan, in the next room.

Net. Here, Mary, come out!—I want to speak to you.

Enter MARY, *with a portrait in her hand*, R. D. F.

Mary. Virginie looks so nice you can't think, quite a lady. Look here, Bob, here's a portrait of her mother—isn't it pretty ?

Net. By Jove ! it's very like the one I saw old snuffy kissing. Lend it me—we'll let him see this before he sees Virginie—he'll think it is the original of the portrait come to him.

Mary. (R.) Oh, how I hope he is married ! Perhaps our trick may succeed.

Net. (C.) And perhaps it may not—we'll be prepared for the worst. I'll stay here, to see how our trick turns out, and you shall run away.

Mary. But I can't run away by myself.

Net. Of course not—Waddilove shall run away with you.

Wad. (L.) I run away with her! I'll do no such thing—I've no objection to apples, or even eggs—but I don't feel myself equal to running away with a young woman.

Net. You've only to go as far as the Six Bells—tip the ostler, and mention my name—he'll let you into his little room over the stable. If I find old snuffy has a wife, you can return; if he hasn't, we'll light a pan of charcoal, and stop up all the key holes. [*Embraces* MARY, R. C.

Wad. (R.) I beg you'll not include me in the charcoal business—anything else to oblige you—but I will not be smothered.

Mary. Well, I'll go, but I'm so frightened.

Net. Waddy, remember you're a man of honour; if you dare to forget it, I'll give you such a thrashing.

Wad. Oh, Mary is quite safe under my care. [*Aside.*] My affections are all bespoke for that interesting orphan. [*Exeunt* R. 1 E.

SCENE IV.—*The School Room*—BOYS *discovered making a great noise—a form* R., *a long school-desk* L.—TOURBILLON *seated at his desk* C.

Tour. Silence !—si-lence !—Sacré ! Brigands, hold ze tongue to all of you. Is it then Chaos, Babel, de school ?

Enter NETTLES, *without being seen, he takes his seat slyly at desk* L.

—Ah, mon dieu ! what a miserable is de master of a school. Oh, happy Abbé de L'Epee ! he taught only de deafs and de dumbs. Mais, courage—de la resignation and du tabac. [*Takes snuff.*] Ah ! now for de premier class—dicté and translation—de first class—it is Nettles. Ici de first class—comment ! he does not come, de first class. [*Sees* NETTLES *very intent on a book inside a large dictionary.*] Tiens, tiens ! for once I catch him at his book. What is dat he study so hard ? [*Goes up and seizes the book* BOB *is reading—spells the title*] J-A-C-K—Jack—Sheppard. Ah, les vols !—du sang !—des horreurs !—Oh !

Net. (L.) Please, Sir !

Tour. (C.) Oh, he is then a demon, dis Nettles !

Net. Please, Sir !

Tour. Ah, I shall read you Jack Sheppard. [*He boxes his ears, then takes the large book and draws forward chair to* C.] Attention ! Monsieur de la premier classe !—dat which I say into English, you shall put him in French. [*Sits and dictates*—NETTLES *writing on slate, making a scratching with a pencil.*] "To hold a dialogue whatever at table, at dinner. Give me some bread; some meat; some cream; some fish; some mustard; some apple-pie; some cheese; some plum pudding; some vinegar; some custard——'

Net. [*Laughing.*] Oh, Lord!—I never!

Tour. What have you then to shout so—eh?

Net. Please, Sir, I was thinking what a precious digestion the gentleman would have.

Tour. [*pulling his ears.*] Ah! you permit yourself remarks, petit monstre! Your slate, dat I may correct de one, two, tree, eight, four, twenty blunder you sall make in tree line. [*Takes slate.*] Maintenant au Telemaque—begin. [*Reads.*] "Calypson ne pouvait se consoler du départ d'Ulysse"—continue.

Net. [*Translating.*] "Calypso," Calypso—"ne pouvait," could not—"se consoler," console herself—"du départ"——

Tour. Departure—for the departure of Ulysse.

Net. [*Mimicking.*] For the departure of Ulysse. "Elle se promenait," she walked herself—"souvent," often—"seule sur le gazon fleuri," [*stealthily consulting dictionary,*] on the flowery bachelor.

Tour. Oh, dieu! What he read now? où ça bachelor?

Net. Here it is in the dictionary, Sir—"garçon, a boy—a bachelor."

Tour. Ah! petit drôle. You see not den de "r;" dere it is, "garçon, boy;" here it is—"gazon, turf"—she walked herself frequently, on ze flowery turf.

Net. [*Imitating.*] On ze flowery turf. "Les yeux," her eyes—"tournés," turned—"vers," worms——

Tour. Oh! ce'st trop! he is then an imbecile. [*Rises.*

Net. Here it is, in the diction——

[*Presents dictionary*—TOURBILLON *dashes it out of his hand.*

During the above, SCRAGGS *sticks a pin into* TOURBILLON'S *seat.*

Tour. Enough like dat! Quelle traduction! I ask you a leetle—Is it permitted to listen to translation like dat? [*Flings himself back in his chair, the pin sticks into him—he jumps up.*] Dieu de Dieu! I am impale! It is den here Turquie—dey are den savages—dese boys. Who have done dis? Who have dared to stick a pin—oh? behind my back? Ah! que ça pique.

Enter DOGGETT, L. 1.

Dog. (L.) Here's a lady wants to see Monsieur Tourbillon.

Tour. (R. C.) Comment! a lady! Sans doubt de moder of a pupil—quel moment—say to her de Docteur Swiss is absent.

Dog. Oh! she don't want him; she wants you particularly; she's a furrin lady.

Tour. Eh! What you say? Foreign—is she—par hazard—is she from France? [*Eagerly.*

Dog. [*Looks to* NETTLES *for instructions, who telegraphs him to say yes.*] Oh? yes—in course—Monsieur.

Tour. A lady to see me from France? What a tremblement dat

word give to my heart; if it should be some news—mais—non—non Did she give no message, no name?

Dog. Oh! yes—the name of the place the bacca comes from—Virginie.

Tour. Virginie—dat name!

Net. [*Aside.*] He has a wife; and we've hit on the right name. Capital!

Tour. And noting else; no message—eh?

Dog Here's her pictur; she said you'd know it.

[TOURBILLON, *seizing portrait, gives a cry, and sinks fainting against* DOGGETT—*he places him in chair,* C.

Net. Now, then, come along, Mrs. T.

Dog. Here she is, Sir.

Enter VIRGINIE, L. 1 E.

[*Exit* DOGGETT.

Vir. How I tremble! [*Sees* TOURBILLON.] Oh, he is dead! What have you donè?

Net. By Jove, h[illegible] has fainted! This is getting past a joke.

Vir. Poor old man! But why did he faint him[illegible]

Net. That's what I want to know. [illegible] oner saw the portrait you lent Mary, than he gave a cry, and went off slap, as you see. Here, bring water, salts, everything.

Vir. No, no! See, he breathes again; de co[illegible]r return to his lip; see—[*As she looks earn[illegible] into his face, she starts back.*] Ah, his face come to me like a drea[illegible]n, half lost. Oh, if it co[illegible]— [*Faintly.*

Net. Hallo! don't you go and f[illegible], [illegible] least till the old gentleman's better.

Vir. (L. C.) No, no! you would not be so cruel to bring fader and child togeder thus—that cannot be—it cannot be.

Net. (L.) Who? [*Aside.*] I begin to think I've been behaving very like a brute

Vir. He is so like papa, only dis poor old face is pale and sad—his was so bright wiz life, and health, and joy! Oh, see—he revive—he will speak to me perhaps.

Tour. [*Slowly reviving.*] Oh, suis je? Is it a dream? Virginie!

[*He suddenly sees her face, seizes her arm, and holds her at arms length.*

—Oh, ciel! Virginie! Speak to me dat I die not in dis struggle of hope and fear. [*Suddenly looking at portrait.*] Dis portrait——

Vir. Was de last gift of my dying moder.

Tour. [*Bursting into a passion of mingled joy and grief.*] Oh. Dieu, Dieu! [*Opens his arms.*] Ma fille! Ma fille! [*Sinks into chair.*

Vir. Mon père! [*Falling on her knees and embracing him.*

Tour. [*After a long and affectionate embrace, gazing proudly and fondly upon her.*] How she is beautiful; but how did you come at me?

Vir. (R. C.) Dis leetle gentleman——

Tour. (C.) Comment! dis enragé of a Nettles. Oh, to my arms, brave boy. [*Seizes him, to embrace him.*] How sall I tank you for restoring to me my child?

Net. (L. C.) Oh don't, Sir, don't—I don't deserve it! I'm a brute—an unfeeling wretch! I did it all for a trick. [illegible] But if I'd known she was your daughter, I'd sooner have cut off my right hand than played such a trick! I've been at the bottom of all your sufferings, Sir—the pin in the chair, and the devil in the snuff-box—and I can't look on your poor old face, and see the tears in *her* eyes—without—feeling—that—I deserve to be flogged—within—an—inch of my life! [*Sobbing.*

Tour. Do not afflict yourself at dat. Ze devil—he is blowed away! Ze pin—no, he prick always a leetle! And my child is here! I pardon you! [*Shakes his hand.*

Enter DOGGETT, *with a packet,* L.

Dog. A letter for Master Nettles.

Net. [*Takes the packet and opens it.*] Yes, it's from uncle George. [*Reads.*] "Name—title—estates." Huzza!—huzza!—huzza! Here's a go! Huzza! [*Seizes* TOURBILLON, *and dances him round.*

Tour. Ah—rest yourself—tranquil! [*Breaks away.*] Is he mad?

Net. No, no—[illegible] pardon, Monsieur. I'll tell you all about it, if I can. I was—[illegible]

Enter SWISH *at back,* [illegible] C.

—reading the paper this morning, when I saw an advertisement, saying that if you applied at [illegible]4 Chancery-lane, you'd hear——

Swish. (L. C.) Hold your tongue. [*Advances.*

Net. (C.) I [illegible] I will tell my story. You'd hear of something greatly to your advantage. So, I wrote to my uncle George, the lawyer, and here's his letter; and you're restored to your title of Count, and the domains of the family! Shout, boys! shout!

Boys. Huzzah! huzzah!

Swish (L. C.) [*Aside.*] The murder's out. All my plans ruined. I'd best put a good face on it! [*Aloud.*] I assure you, my dear Count, I was hurrying to you with the same gratifying intelligence, and it was only my desire to be the bearer of it, that made me anxious to stop our young friend Nettles. [*Aside.*] I wish his neck was broken.

Tour. [*Bowing coldly to* SWISH.] I appreciate your kindness; you already shewed it to me this morning——

Swish. Oh!

Tour. I tink, just after you read the newspaper. If I rejoice dat I recover title and wealth, it is not for myself; it is for you, ma fille, ma Virginie, dat your youth shall be rich, happy, and honored, to bless de old age of de fader who adores you.

Vir. And for dis, also, must we tank dis bon leetle Monsieur. Oh, merci! a tousand times merci!

Tour. Ah, embrassez-moi all ze both! [*They embrace.*

Enter NUBBLES, *dragging in* WADDILOVE *and* MARY, D. F. L. C.

Wad. He's embracing the orphan!

Swish. [*Aside.*] Here's somebody I *can* thrash, at last. [*Aloud.*] What's the meaning of this?

www.ingramcontent.com/pod-product-compliance
Lightning Source LLC
LaVergne TN
LVHW011145110826
845150LV00008B/2526
9781418191986